LEGAL NOTICE

The Distributer has strived to be essentially as exact and finish as conceivable in the production of this report, despite the way that he warrants or addresses never that the items inside are precise because of the quickly changing nature of the Web.

This book is a sound judgment manual for chasing after riches. In down to earth exhortation books, similar to whatever else throughout everyday life, there are no certifications of pay made.

Pursuers are forewarned to answer on their own judgment about their singular conditions to as needs be act.

This book isn't planned for use as a wellspring of legitimate, business, bookkeeping or monetary exhortation. All pursuers are educated to look for administrations regarding skillful experts in lawful, business, bookkeeping, and money field.

Any apparent affronts of explicit individuals or associations are inadvertent.

This guide is written in Times New Roman for simple perusing. You are urged to print this book

Table of Contents

Preface 4
Introduction 5
The 5 Principles to Unlocking Wealth 5
It Can Never Happen? 6
Pursuing Wealth 8
Has This Happened to You? 8
The Ladder to Success 10
Formula to Success 13
The Basic Steps 14
Steps to Personal Wealth 16
Achieving Your Goal 18
The Keys to Success 19
The Power of Thoughts 22
Factors That Bring Inertia 25
The Risk Factor 28
What You Must Avoid 30
The Inevitable Mistakes 33
The Law of Success 36
Time to Learn Who You Are 38
The Need for Change 39
Understanding Failure 42
The Final Goal 44
Paving Your Path to Success 45
The Law of Prosperity 48

Power of Words 50
The Power of Unconditional Love 52
Conclusion 54

Preface

The Distributer has strived to be essentially as exact and finish as conceivable in the production of this report, despite the way that he warrants or addresses never that the items inside are precise because of the quickly changing nature of the Web.

This book is a sound judgment manual for chasing after riches. In down to earth exhortation books, similar to whatever else throughout everyday life, there are no certifications of pay made.

Pursuers are forewarned to answer on their own judgment about their singular conditions to as needs be act.

This book isn't planned for use as a wellspring of legitimate, business, bookkeeping or monetary exhortation. All pursuers are educated to look for administrations regarding skillful experts in lawful, business, bookkeeping, and money field.

Any apparent affronts of explicit individuals or associations are inadvertent.

This guide is written in Times New Roman for simple perusing. You are urged to print this book

Introduction

One of the most troublesome focuses to accommodate in life is the paradox that enduring exists in this world. Enduring is prominent.

Obviously, what is similarly significant is understanding that the obtaining and ownership of abundance isn't a ruler that actions one's joy. On the off chance that bliss really was to be found in materials, every one of the people who experience the 'adventure' of it by coming into contact with the item would notice a similar proportion of happiness.

Throughout everyday life, men are constantly spurred by two inescapable driving forces of repugnance - from distress and hankering to looking for satisfaction and outright satisfaction.

In the mission to embrace all joy, he is constrained to pursue the pleasant and pleasing, while at the same time facing the alternate extremes, he keeps away from bothersome items and unpleasant conditions.

The truth of the matter is this: since forever ago, all achievers cognizant or subliminally have utilized five standards, which are normal to outright advance in all parts of life.

The 5 Principles to Unlocking Wealth

These principles are a key to unlocking amazing cache of wealth, abundance and success. They are all centered on our true innate qualities, which as a matter of fact are universal and have a spiritual basis. These principles are:

- Truth
- Righteousness
- Peace
- Love, and
- Non-violence

The act of these Excellencies will empower anybody to advance in existence no doubt.

The explanation is basic.

These general standards are alluring and obviously, they structure the foundations of the set of rules. You can't turn out badly rehearsing the significance to virtues, implicit sets of principles and submitting to the Law of Nature in your quest for Riches.

In the approaching pages, you will find the objective of arriving at independence from the rat race while simultaneously, obtaining the ideal craft of satisfaction through the comprehension that the proportion of happiness isn't 'straightforwardly' corresponding to simply money related riches.

This succinct, exact and focused original copy investigates roads that are undoubtedly going to completely change yourself to improve things.

Not at all like numerous different books on a similar subject, this original copy dives on branches of knowledge pertinent to parts of your own life and development that I can ensure will welcome back that grin all over. It is clear, engaged or more each of the intelligible book, which you will appreciate.

It Can Never Happen?

While cynicism cautions us of perils prowling before our own special eyes, hopefulness might drive us into misleading security. Cynicism ought to just be viewed as starting and not a last quandary in any circumstance - this is the **initial step** to progress.

Consistently, we have been exposed to occurrences that are upsetting, and profound inside us we 'understand' the likely risks and dangers encompassing us, and the 'voice' inside resolutely dismisses this undermining circumstance standing up to us, as such on the grounds that we neglect to perceive this 'voice' inside us our psychological sticking to the external world withdraws us from the internal voice of 'TRUTH' subsequently tossing us absolutely of the tracks figuratively speaking.

The **second move** toward progress and abundance is to persuade yourself regarding the significance of discretion, mindfulness and self-control.

We should pay attention to the voice inside and understand the presence of the natural power or the Unique Determination - the strong power communicating through the brain, body and the keenness! Subsequently the subsequent step qualifies that you foster confidence in what you can do and accomplish as well as above all creating confidence in yourself (your natural, innate and idle characteristics).

Stage three expects that through consistent watchfulness, utilizing the influence of knowledge, self examination and thoughtfulness and through cautious comprehension and utilization of these ideas, you can figure out how to live past the requests of the brain in anything climate you track down yourself - this will qualify you to carry out and embrace the way to riches.

A free lunch can't exist. Assuming you prefer not to invest any energy/exertion however love to accomplish achievement, you should rethink your perspectives

So to accomplish the last option, you need to do the previous and the reasonable thought is to figure out what truly gives us joy and afterward see whether it is feasible to bring in cash from getting it done.

"If you do not start you will not succeed."

Pursuing Wealth

The assertion 'flurry makes squander' stands genuine even today, and generally, a few of us will more often than not feel baffled when we can't satisfy our beliefs and the guidelines we set for ourselves constantly.

On different events, we might feel that had we taken the test that came our direction that maybe things might well have improved, yet there is likewise the likelihood that in our over nervousness to arrive at the objective we make a good attempt and wear ourselves out completely!

Has This Happened to You?

The inquiry that presently still needs to be posed to how would we start, how might we make progress throughout everyday life?

Indeed, old buddy, have confidence that this book has been composed to address this question sufficiently, killing disarray or abnormalities at all.

There are numerous methodologies that one can utilize and different means through which you can furrow yourself to accomplishing the objective. One ongoing idea in every one of them is self-conviction, pomposity or trustworthiness and moral living (in words, deeds, contemplations and activities) relating to your way of life - this is Stage four.

In any business the accentuation on moral and moral guidelines positions the most elevated, and this ought not be disregarded or neglected.

The best way to accomplish poise, equilibrium or balance even after you become the most well off individual is to have your feeling of understanding the genuine pith of life.

Nothing in life is consistent. Life is truly changing and things that appear to have presence today might stop existing tomorrow and this is a reality that you - and every other person - should figure out how to acknowledge.

Stage five, when you find something significant and wonderful, the regular propensity is to impart it to other people.

In the accompanying parts what you will find are the genuine ways of making total progress, and this is a book that will permit you to release your natural characteristics to the front, subsequently permitting you to receive the advantages and the benefits that a huge number of individuals all around the world at the present time are getting a charge out of in light of the fact that they have become well off.

Following the aide inside the approaching pages, and it is my earnest accept that each individual can possibly prevail throughout everyday life.

"Wealth is more than just money."

The Ladder to Success

It is the honor of man to accomplish all over significance, and actually achievement ought to be one's propensity. Man is basically awesome, and accordingly endless are the potential outcomes that lie torpid in him.

To draw out the absolute best from the inside, a daily existence coordinated and impeccably focused for the revelation of the possibilities that untruth prowling inside us, is a day to day existence very much spent.

The imperative point isn't the number of abilities each on of us has, yet the significance ought to be centered around the amount of our current gifts, traits and capacities are we arranged to create, exploit, investigate and execute in our regular routines.

The inquiry you should pose, is whether you are utilizing no less than one extraordinary ability lying innate inside you? The one preeminent central chief is to comprehend that all our prosperity completely relies on ourselves

The most effective way to be content is to do the things that you normally love and appreciate doing - something that you are totally energetic about! Similarly the most effective way to succeed and become rich is to make sure that you accomplish the things you have truly wanted to look for throughout everyday life. This will expect that you execute your endeavors in to exercises that will permit you to quantify achievement.

For example the straightforward method for making sense of this is to think about the accompanying model: on the off chance that you begin to appreciate for craftsmanship, painting, and attracting the best approach is to look for direction on ways of entering contests, and ways of presenting your fine art through displays (move toward exhibitions straightforwardly and go home on a deal or return premise) or artistic work distributers' or in any event, uncovering your ability by entering occasional fairs where you will track down a huge get-together of a wide range of retailers.

You might need to add different various kinds of topics to your specialty portfolio to boost your abilities to contact a crowd of people all over with interests in various topics/subjects.

Contact gatherings, discussions and even Web newsgroups and investigate different roads, (for example, picture takers, photograph and outlining displays, expressions committees and government associations that give assistance including credits and so on) that will permit you to move forward your enquiry - the thought is to seek after the objective tirelessly and with an inspirational perspective.

To the extent that your topic/topic is concerned post questions, surveys, studies, and figures out the thing individuals are searching for, and afterward basically track down the need and fill it.

Every single will help, however it is the power expected to get the force rolling and that is the central issue. Another helpful point isn't to simply attempt, attempt and to keep attempting - rather foster a demeanor by which you DO what you have chosen to seek after, execute and apply the systems displayed in this book.

At long last don't stop at that - keep confidence and respect no loss.

Whenever you have chosen to place the 'plan' right into it, ensure that it is kept lighted and gleaming... dismissals and disillusionments should not the slightest bit diminish your expectation, progress and your longing to progress. Individuals who have prevailed notwithstanding all the difficulty, agony and battle have enlivened incalculable millions all over the planet - it is time you too set a model for others to emulate your example.

You should recollect that the techniques utilized by various people in obtaining abundance might be particular, however the objective is normal to all, and the means discussed before are active your devices to your general achievement.

Extremely amazing self control is required to grow inside, and the requirement for two most significant properties, in particular boldness and certainty are fundamental fixings. Accordingly destitution and flourishing doesn't be guaranteed to rely upon information entirely (for example business discernment, advertising procedures, etc) yet it absolutely relies upon the three C's and they are character, imagination and your natural abilities.

Boldness and certainty alone can achieve special change while the contrary will just get a lot of distress and hopelessness seasons of trouble and emergency. In any case, in spite of life's concerns we ought to oppose deterrents and obstructions and as such continually help ourselves to remember the preeminent innate

or on the other hand natural power which we as a whole groups and which we can all effectively foster through profound understanding. Subsequently disregarding our capacities and potential for fostering the individual power that we really want for going through inner self breaking encounters requires gigantic mettle and discipline, and I make sense of for you in this book on how you could accomplish this present time and place.

Without these characteristics you are bound to fall flat, and that is the justification for why a huge piece of individuals feel miserable in light of the fact that they got into contest or they essentially surrendered under tension, through absence of self-boldness and dynamic determination.

At the point when our dreams and assumptions are not satisfied, there is an inclination for us to return to our prior ways - the void we experience can be generally irritating and we can't overlook it for eternity. A great deal of the time what precisely happens is that anything that great we embrace throughout everyday life, it doesn't mean we will proceed. This isn't on the grounds that an unthinkable discipline is required but since we need mental fortitude and certainty we are overpowered with negative demeanor - this leaves everything speechless!

The underlying eruption of excitement starts to blur, and what appeared to be so brilliant turns into a danger a predicament and an issue. The psyche dominates and questions overcome raising a large number of questions whether the entire thought or idea is beneficial - a contention results, the brain says the a certain something and the insight and our instinct urges us to follow the way to 'achievement'.

Indeed, even before we start the excursion the end is unavoidable, in light of the fact that we unsure genuine way to follow. Achievement lies in what you think about it not what you 'think' it should be (don't fantasize achievement).

So how might we get everything rolling?

Formula to Success

What you think and how you then, at that point, act is the game changer that will assist you with finding the objective of achievement. These two ascribes are significant together with a bunch of predictable standards, which you see everything through to completion. Considerations in light of reason are a strong impetus to begin any response, and when you set off; you will before long understand that boldness is the basic goodness required for a person to navigate the rough street.

Snags are normal, and they are a way to the wellspring of securing riches, as I'm certain you will concur. Tirelessness, persistence and determination should be rehearsed strictly to arrive at the objective and to conquer the impediments. Obviously that said, I might now want to call attention to the P's that you ought to dislike.

Try not to tarry, don't imagine that you know everything lastly don't draw out your 'venture(s)'. Be ready to battle the hindrances that might defy you, yet seek after your objective and permit your expected self discipline to prevail.

In any circumstance throughout everyday life, it is unequivocally critical to stay reasonable, regardless of all the 'ups and the downs' that we are probably going to confront. Recall life is dualistic ordinarily - the front-side and the opposite sides of a similar coin to just put it. I'm constrained to add that however we realize that the past is the reason and the present is the impact, it is plainly obvious that with time the actual current turns into the reason concerning what's to come.

There is an exceptionally profound importance entangled in this sentence structure, and on the off chance that you can relate this to progress, then one might say that in the event that we brilliantly live in the logical self-restraint, we can turn into the modelers of our own future.

The Basic Steps

The accompanying rules will assist you with clearing a magnificent way to your definitive achievement.

The means are extremely easy to carry out in your regular routine.

1. Live life to the fullest and what you are great at.

2. Be ready to learn and to be positive (inspiration and excitement).

3. Be an imaginative person.

4. Be ready to put away cash as well as your time, exertion and assets, as well.

I referenced cash - this doesn't imply that you need to contribute a huge aggregate to turn into a mogul or well off.

5. You should be focused in having laid out objectives and targets. Recall that industriousness is the way to progress.

6. You should be ready to actually deal with your time.

7. As you develop, figure out how to offer back what you store up to the general public. I call this generosity.

You should have a strong vision - one in which you 'see' yourself having accomplished achievement. Extraordinary individuals of the at various times make sure that they arrive at this sought after position, by utilizing these fundamental stages.

Notwithstanding, notice in sync 2 I purposely utilized the word 'learn', and that too understandably. Life is the best instructor, hence you should acknowledge demands constantly (utilizing the force of separation) and subsequently thus you should learn by means of its everlasting standards the eminent teaching it has uncovered with the progression of time. This implies that you should act when all is good and well.

Activity is unquestionably significant and features achievement - the two are interchangeable honestly. To succeed activity is required yet the fundamental fixing is the way serious you are. Being excessively intense can destroy your undertaking, so the point is to have A great time.

Any discipline will require association and precision. You should as I referenced in the acquaintance be ready with pay attention to your internal voice however much you can. This implies that as opposed to being too subject to your family, companions, etc (not that this is awful) start to have confidence in your own abilities.

Independent and endeavor to learn and succeed. Frequently, disappointments may simply result from examples where we have quit practicing our own perspectives, or we have become too subject to other people'.

Achievement isn't some mysterious that you need to look for or uncover to arrive at your objective; it is fairly the comprehension or the acknowledgment factor that you create concerning what you truly need throughout everyday life. Instinct, mental fortitude, abilities, information, difficulties and potential open doors are a portion of the ideas that decide the qualities of individuals who appreciate riches. Any errand performed with the right soul will give you triumph. Mental disposition will give you achievement, however bad demeanor, lethargy and working reluctantly will bring about disappointment.

Try not to anticipate a lot in too short a period; however your methodology ought to be positive and execute your errand with outright flawlessness, giving specific consideration to your long haul goal(s). This implies that you approach your obligation with concentrated energy and you execute your arrangements uprightly. This ought to be your way of thinking of life.

To start another endeavor, it essentially vital that you understand the accompanying, which I need to say is significant. You need to see the value in the way that to begin a business you really want to familiarize yourself with the term income. Venture as a capital is a necessity, yet more critically it is the idea of reasonability of the undertaking that makes the biggest difference.

Steps to Personal Wealth

Direction is maybe the hardest move toward move past with in your mission to start the excursion to riches. The issue is until you don't dig profound inside yourself to open your inborn characteristics odds are you will be ambivalent and reluctant. This is essentially on the right track accordingly, yet as a general rule this 'feeling' may not permit you to boost your maximum capacity.

There is no confidential to releasing your all out potential - the 'secret' lies in your readiness to pay attention to your internal voice. The drive to immediately jump all over a decent chance that comes your direction is by embraced the undertaking in a deliberate manner.

Sit discreetly, quiet your faculties and considerations, and ponder profoundly on the topic being referred to. Try not to bounce into anything immediately in light of the fact that the thought appears to be positive. Most things show up generally excellent in the underlying stage, yet thinking, arranging and time are an essential. Frequently it is something inside that will instruct you. The mystery isn't really from without, yet can be obtained from the inside.

Endeavoring to give your all consistently is the little mystery that will assist you with gathering riches. Creative mind (I mean useful creative mind) which is the ability to picture is a significant figure innovative idea - yet as you will value you cannot do this without a solid will, or more this staff of perception must be matured into firm conviction and conviction.

1. You should really want to accomplish your objective of acclaim - this is rule number one

2. Be ready to deal with cash effectively as for spending plan, use and obligation and additionally responsibility.

3. Try not to spend more than you are expected to and spend short of what you make.

4. Individual issues, including compulsion not exclusively to drugs and so forth, can be ruinous. This is something that should be dealt with from the very beginning.

5. Sort out ways of financial planning or more all start to set aside cash. You should play brilliant and get your needs totally right.

In any endeavor, all things considered, you might confront a ton of threat, a long ways from an optimistic circumstance. Over assumptions, over hopefulness and the inclination to 'wish' that things run as expected, can and frequently may prompt disappointment.

Subsequently as referenced before arranging is vital to your prosperity. Obviously different elements that one necessity to consider likewise is over work and weariness. In the desire to make your millions, the likelihood is that you will end up being a baffled wreck and become very miserable - this won't be useful in your advancement or pursuit to riches.

Achieving Your Goal

At the point when you continue declining to acknowledge disappointment, realize that the item you have decided to accomplish will appear through the powerful resolve.

Considerations can be inconceivably incredible assets, and in the event that you will carry out this heavenly gift, you make certain to accomplish your objective. On the off chance that you grip to a specific idea with dynamic determination, it expects a substantial outward structure.

Right now is an ideal opportunity to close up the negative qualities intrinsic as propensities, absence of solid determination, absence of certainty, reluctance and wrong mentality towards life overall. You have inside you the ability to achieve all that you need, that power lies in the will. The main driver of disappointment in life is absence of fixation - don't accumulate yourself with thoughts, ideas and methodologies at the same time in the very desire to succeed. Start gradually and be reliable in your objective setting plan.

Concentrate on each thing in turn, and don't permit your Brain to go in a condition of 'over drive'. There is a logical approach to using fixation, and the enchanted word is to resist the urge to panic, while you play out the entirety of your obligations with the right speed.

Try not to rush and make confusion, yet rather deliberately and carefully concentration and focus your entire brain on anything you attempt, and the significant thing is to keep your psyche adaptable.

When you realize that you are truly in good shape and on the way to accomplishing your objective, do practice care, taking everything into account. It is frequently extremely simple to engage with a venture to such an extent that you can overdo it in idealizing whatever you are doing.

You should focus on your work or more all regard and honor the worth of time - don't burn through your time and your life!

The Keys to Success

As I have referenced the climate assumes a gigantic part as it is very unavoidable - especially our inward climate.

A quiet loosened up individual is undeniably bound to come out a champ in a difficult circumstance than his/her partner - an individual who his apprehensive disappointed and sporadic. The previous has his faculties completely related to the climate in which he puts himself.

Be that as it may, the fretful individual doesn't grasp the climate and subsequently causes problems. The watchwords are concentration, focus and care in anything that you do throughout everyday life.

1. Foster a distinct and an obvious objective/point.

2. Draw up an insightful functional arrangement/program.

3. Watch your wellbeing. Without wellbeing there is no genuine riches.

4. You should moderate your energy.

5. Tell the truth in your life (in words, deeds, considerations and activities).

6. Stick to temperance and embrace great standards.

7. Ponder ideal characters and look for strength from their way of thinking.

8. Look for divine direction and be honest.

9. Try to assist and serve others with appreciation.

10. Continuously think positive and put stock in the force of God.

Extraordinary reasoning is to be sure the way to progress. Set out an arrangement to accomplish your objective and intentionally ruminate over the significance of this arrangement and get it going.

From days of yore incredible individuals from varying backgrounds have arisen as evident victors and the explanation for this is preparing the brain for joy.

Moral discipline is fundamental, especially self-control.

Every individual is one of a kind. What is great for individual A may not be reasonable for individual B. Nonetheless, it must be stressed that all can appreciate quietude, isolation and quiet, and to be straightforward each individual regardless old enough, position, doctrine, variety, sex has at some stage or one more had harmony.

Subsequent to finding through experimentation strategy, you can decide the exact method for making your brain body complex and hence achieve extraordinary levels.

Reflection may not be powerful for all, however that doesn't imply that you don't ad lib such strategies as and when required.

Be methodical, and your main objective ought to be to utilize strategies that give you achievement and joy.

Our intellectual capacities decide our activities, and it is very clear that the psyche ought to be restrained and repressed. Steady cautiousness is important and nonstop preparation of the brain will clear the way to extreme achievement.

Try not to succumb to the directs of your psyche!

Hopeful, courageous and respectable beliefs have a strong and elevating impact upon the body. Energy with purposeful perfectly tuned self-application in euphoric mind-set and outright positive thinking is the mysterious way to abundance for every single extraordinary man.

The Power of Thoughts

The first section featured the significance of developing right disposition and creating confidence in what you try to accomplish throughout everyday life.

Nothing in life is unimaginable, except if you think it so. Contemplations are surprising 'bundles' of energy and on the off chance that you steadily stick to a specific idea with the powerful self control, there is not an obvious explanation for why this thought can't appear as indicated by the outline you have made.

Prior I momentarily referenced by making sense of how an individual keen on craftsmanship can move forward his/her capacities to succeed throughout everyday life. I will currently utilize a similar guide to delineate the force of thought. A craftsman fosters a thought of making a composition or a drawing of a delightful scene.

The manner of thinking starts a progression of thoughts and the craftsman consequently utilizes these plans to deliver the skeleton work, which permits him/her to ultimately finish the last masterpiece as indicated by the psychological diagram made at first. A simple manner of thinking permits the craftsman to make the work of art!

This creation is in itself a logical chief in view of the General Law Of Creation. It is the source from which everything shows. It is in every one of us, and it can surely be tapped on the off chance that you are simply ready to try it out. The mystery is not exactly confidential, however it is a mother lode inside all of us and we reserve the option to utilize it most viably.

Is it false that when you see somebody so exceptionally blissful and thrilled, your brain finds out the latest with the cheer and you find that there is a grin all over?

The contemplations are so firmly joined with the psyche. Assuming that the considerations are quiet the brain is quiet. In any part of life, be it beginning a business, landing your most memorable position or getting hitched, the relationship of psyche and believed is chief.

Efficiently, consequently we should prepare and train the psyche for right reasoning and persistent movement, and hence have right comprehension of what you truly need throughout everyday life, and how this will add to the solid dynamism in your journey and what you at last look for - your way to progress and abundance will become benevolent, significant and achievable!

Individuals with specific characteristics are attractively drawn in, and such characteristics are called positive characteristics. These characteristics are available in every last one of us, however they are not summoned or obviously comprehended. We understand what love, consideration, fortitude and satisfaction mean, these are respectable temperance, and we moreover remember them as characteristics we appreciate in others

Notwithstanding knowing this, when we act we act compromising goals. The explanation for this is that we are never consistent with our own selves - we are continually acting and setting up a 'show' to satisfy everybody around us, however ourselves!

It is difficult, debilitating and very anguishing not to be your actual self.

You might shout in dismay, and sat what has this have to do with abundance and thriving? I recognize your anxiety, however I submissively demand that you pause for a little while, and in the quietness of the night ruminate over this point profoundly. I would like you then to execute what I referenced above by acting naturally.

Notice the progressions that happen with the progression of time, and what you will genuinely find is that when one can bring out into articulation the scent of one's inborn positive characteristics or attributes (of who you truly are), then individuals as well as everything that you have at any point wanted or wanted for will come to you.

"As the thought, so the mind."

To satisfy your put forth objectives and your fantasies, it is important to rehearse what the book frames.

The routine tendency of our thinking designs is at last the game changer, which decides our capacities, gifts and our own qualities. In light of this basic and essential piece of information, one expects that those fortunate few have been brought into the world with the unique ability you need and intensely want to have.

Generally this is valid, however it must be said that nobody is conceived a tycoon - full stop! The significant data lies in the specialty of developing the example that brings achievement. We are what we assume we are.

It is valid when that's what experts say, "Your Contemplations establish the climate".

Contemplations foster character

• Contemplations advance wellbeing

• Contemplations impact the body

• Contemplations can change and shape the future (predetermination)

• Considerations deliver creation

• Considerations impact the physiology and brain research of individuals

• Considerations can bring achievement

• Considerations might actually recuperate the body

Watch your considerations continually. Your encounters and the climate have their 'seat' in considerations.

Your idea, and autosuggestions through reflection and perception strategies should be more grounded than the 'considerations, and when your activities inspire you, realize that you have grasped the specialty of controlling your manners of thinking.

You can achieve anything through the force of thought. Representation utilizes your creative mind to permit yourself to 'picture' your prosperity or accomplishing your sincere objective.

Your psychological considerations or vibrations are extraordinarily strong, in light of the fact that the brain has an unmistakable association with your viewpoints and your activities. Your considerations are inconspicuous energies and have serious areas of strength for a to our cognizance.

Accordingly, steady sustenance of positive contemplations through representation, yoga and reflection will bring concordance, joy, wellbeing and riches!

Factors That Bring Inertia

Above all else is to introspect, and this in a real sense implies that you check out your qualities and propensities.

Frequently, absence of self-examination is the reason for our deficit, and it is the absence of unequivocal, unified exertion and consideration that holds you up to advance and accomplishment of your ideal objective.

Reflection thusly implies reassessment of our psychological barrier and diagnosing lacks by getting rid of negative propensities as propensities, uncertainty, dread, absence of certainty, etc - what we frequently term as disappointments.

The time has come to recharge so that by evacuating this multitude of negativities from your life the genuine satisfaction with the enthusiasm to advance becomes conspicuous and immovably established.

The best adversary that prevents us from progressing in life other than detachment, absence of certainty and feeling of inadequacy is Dread. Dread will in a real sense prevent us from pushing ahead - as a matter of fact we won't actually satisfy our very plan to succeed. The most effective way to battle dread is to rehearse profound breathing activities, and consistently intellectually certify that you are under the assurance of the preeminent character of godhead, and empower your contemplations with good sentiments.

Deliberately remove the seeds of dread from inside by intense fixation upon mental fortitude, and shift your attention to a level that permits you to completely see the value in that you are past any sort or sort of harming. Dread comes from the heart, so make you inexpressibly pleased with Adoration, and when you feel unsettled unwind, quiet down and inhale musically, unwinding with every exhalation.

Obviously there is one more issue, which I accept, is the significant reason for dissatisfaction and thusly hosing our capacity to succeed throughout everyday life. It is, what I call 'covetous of results without the will to invest the energy'. I have by and by fizzled due to such a negative viewpoint - and I'm the first to straightforwardly concede this.

Presently this is where the point I made above becomes more clear.

Disappointment, distress, disease and deficiencies are regular possibilities when the Law of Nature is broken.

Offense and infringement of the everlasting Law of nature brings wretchedness. As people we have the capacities to shape, right and transform us, objectives and predetermination.

The best hindrance that you will at any point meet in your life is your prompt climate. Assuming that anything you should change that - you might have seen that I began this book sounding marginally skeptical and to some degree over wary, significantly less somewhat negative - the excellent justification behind this will now become obvious.

The climate that I just referenced can be characterized into two, to be specific the inward and the external. It is these two fields of climate that you should look out for.

Every one of your encounters come from your brain stuff - or the inward climate (considerations). What you see through the entirety of your faculties from the external will similarly shape your future.

In this way the significant point here is to oversee your considerations. My idea to you is to be careful with your inward climate more so than your external climate. For instance you might have coincidentally found an extraordinary self-start venture opportunity that is possibly great and spot on for you in each perspective.

You are cheerful, and very ready to try it out... yet by and large something about this business 'prevents' you from proceeding it. There might be a few explanations behind this, yet I'm extremely inquisitive to get familiar with the significant explanation. Rest guaranteed it can't be the cash (since it is affordable for you), nor could it at any point be a promotion (since it has evidently worked for thousands with tributes to affirm).

So what is it I wonder? Ponder this point, and you will most likely reached an ideal resolution... and shockingly it is, the brain stuff - the culprit.

To prevail in life you should start by amending your thinking designs, since it is the organization of your viewpoints and the proclivity you have for them that will decide your destiny.

"Thoughts express through the physical body."

The Risk Factor

Without straying from the topic, I might want to remind you what I referenced in the beginning phases of the book in regards to the dualistic idea of life.

Can any anyone explain why certain individuals are so fortunate but others fall behind in the battle to succeed?

To answer this convincingly it is actually quite significant that larger part of individuals have the idea that princely individuals have something extraordinary which they clearly need - This isn't correct obviously, but what makes one individual more extravagant than the other is generally subject to the decision or the choice taken, combined with the risk(s) recognized through the more prominent comprehension of the force of segregation, and the capacity to gauge and adjust the sizes of your instinctive workforce.

Presently the gamble that you take must be one in light of the comprehension that the endeavor you have chosen to seek after has been explored completely. You just leave after stepping through a driving examination for instance once you feel that you are adequately capable to pass it and not in any case.

Accordingly, the gamble that you embrace in such manner must be what I call an educated gamble. All in all, it is one where you have certainty on the thing you are finding yourself mixed up with, and this also depends on data source that you have looked through well.

The way that you are currently perusing this report is to acquire the comprehension on the best way to make monetary progress - consequently this report is in a manner your examination device to empower you to then carry out the procedures and the tips framed to accomplish the objective. The activity taken has consequently come straightforwardly from a source that can be thought of as bona fide, significant and certified

When you feel certain to step through the driving exam with the direction of the driving teacher obviously, you choose to step through the driving exam - this is the ideal method for guaranteeing a positive outcome. I wish to change a point made beforehand and it is tied in with learning.

You should advance continually, on the grounds that to acquire any ability, information and power, you should be ready to **LEARN**.

Responsibility is the indispensable power which you ought to especially become accustomed to from the very beginning. Recollect that there are sure circumstances that you might not have direct control to bring any predictable changes, which might bring about much despair.

Nonetheless, this need not at any point be the case since the main thing is the system or how you control what is going on and eventually the way that well you respond to it

The issue with us is that we will quite often live before and in the future simultaneously. At the point when our intellectual capacity becomes over troubled we become deterred.

The heap is excessively weighty for the brain, so we should confine the heap. At the point when we have a lot to do at one at once, without a moment's delay stop our exercises. The clock ticks on at a standard speed, it can't tick 24 hours away in 60 seconds, nor might you at any point do in one hour what you can do generally really in

24 hours. Live for the now, and the 'future' will deal with itself.

Try not to be covetous or more all don't wear yourself out by 'needing' to turn into a tycoon!

The tables have pivoted, an ever increasing number of individuals are depending on a straightforward simple way of life - without such countless extravagances and less concerns.

The dualistic idea of nature is predominant all over the place - you can't succeed assuming that you work out checks without having sound assets or credit (store) in your ledger, at some point or another you will hit a financial dead end.

Without inward feeling of harmony, the probable hood of running spent', 'bliss, serenity and strength you will become 'bankrupt' intellectually, inwardly, profoundly and genuinely depleted. What a pity it will have all been to come to a mark of unadulterated devastation!

This is the point at which you should harp on the power inside, and intellectually assert your motivation throughout everyday life; you might need to go through some lovely experience so you fail to remember your concerns totally. The point is make too much of nothing, appreciate what you have and be content with what is your due.

What You Must Avoid

It is normal that when the unexpected happens we are undeniably bound to respond in a negative manner. Anyway this need not be thus, the book uncovers ways of accomplishing your objective agreeably and steadily.

Coming up next are a few pointers that will be generally useful:

1. At the point when things turn out badly don't go overboard. Think decidedly and smoothly.

2. Try not to be over critical, and over basic.

3. Make an effort not to disregard what is happening, be careful with the safe place.

4. Insight and strength alone can assist you with conquering quite a bit of life's impending issues.

5. Tackle issues head on.

6. Stay away from eagerness and pride of any sort.

There is a business morals and a money manager ought to rehearse this morals.

The people who are totally fair and honest will prosper in business. Let us by and by consider workmanship as an illustration to feature what has been talked about so far. As we as a whole realize we have intrinsic abilities - inside each and everybody of us lies the storage facility of inactive energy blasting to be 'stirred'.

Allow us to expect that you have the imaginative power, and that being a craftsman for instance you can practically paint and draw any subject or topic.

All good, clearly you have impressive ability as not all craftsmen have this capacity. Since you know about this, you might expect that on the grounds that your fine art is great it can possibly be sold. Valid, however let us believe all factors that should be made into account a stride at a time.

1. You might be an excellent craftsman, however on the off chance that your work doesn't get seen and appreciated, it is of no genuine advantage. It is significant consequently that your work gets seen (through most extreme openness) and the method for doing this is get your name laid out.

This expects that you contact the right sources and move toward specialists who have experienced the 'same' expectation to absorb information so to speak to arrive at the way of flourishing. You should think about contest that might exist in your picked field. You should set up a solid groundwork - this should be possible utilizing the data inside the pages of this book.

2. Your fine art might be extraordinarily lovely, however without understanding the elements of the commercial center your work may not bloom.

3. According to your own viewpoint your work might appear to have extraordinary potential. In any case, it is applicable to see the value in the perspectives on the overall population - at the end of the day your likely purchasers.

Try not to get into the trench that most do, "hearing what we need to hear" this is a kind of preconditioning that can bring untold hopelessness.

4. You should investigate different regions to foster your true capacity. Develop subject class/topic, utilization of different various kinds of media (for example acrylics, oils. Blended media and so on), settling on the most proficient method to advance your work, you might try and need to sell firsts or replicate prints maybe... The potential outcomes

are unending, the inquiry is the means by which decided you are in your journey to succeed.

The brain science of achievement relies upon number of elements, however the one I accept that is most essential is self-conviction. A great many people never get the primary phase of progress since they miss the mark on trademark, which is fundamental.

Such molding frequently originates from your own encounters, yet the causative variable is climate, which has previously been examined. However it is great to be mindful about anything that you do throughout everyday life, it is similarly fundamental that you don't get tangled into the details of the 'interaction', but instead center around the advantages and a definitive prize that it yields.

Commit your objective to making progress by carrying out the five cardinal words starting with the letter D to your prosperity, in particular Commitment, Separation, Discipline, Assurance and Obligation

There is no damage in bringing up issues with respect to proposition that come your direction or even business amazing open doors you expect chasing after. Insofar as these inquiries manage the cost of the relative multitude of answers and that you choose to finish thinking about every one of the variables, then it is just fine.

Be that as it may, when your inquiries nullify the actual point of your request then it turns into a 'endless loop'.

Why, what, where, when, who are words that we frequently use to learn data about all that in life including undertakings - in this way leading to questions.

The inquiry with the word for what reason is a need for it will assist us with making an ideal determination and assist us with beating questions. The issue with this is that in the event that you are not satisfactory about your goal(s), then, at that point, the very question why you wish to try and seek after the endeavor becomes futile.

What you should consider are plausible long haul objectives, advantages and how your initial step to abundance and achievement will empower you to appreciate more prominent levels.

The Inevitable Mistakes

As people we are exceptionally anxious - we frequently become overpowered with bliss, achievement or satisfaction. It is so vital to keep up with your quiet during such occasions, since energy can prompt issues, of which one is over spending.

All things considered, it is additionally very essential to understand that achievement may just 'thump' you back, in that you might become smug and 'choose' to avoid a lot, since you 'have everything'.

This is a horrible stage that you might at any point conceivably get into, and one you should intentionally know about consistently. Nonetheless, the one thing that you should be careful with is the self image complex - don't give yourself image become an obstruction access your undertaking to achieve abundance.

The best medication to stay away from inner self is to ration energy. The energy that has been created and monitored, except if it is coordinated into the right channels, it will be devastating.

We should control our desires, and this is where the specialty of rehearsing balance in life turns into a fundamental apparatus to your prosperity. Inactive talk is one single element that can obliterate your craving to succeed.

Keep in mind, that individuals around you and the organization you have will decide your future achievement - you might burn through valuable time, yet everyone around you will aggravate it, they will add to in general wastage of your own time.

Hence as the platitude goes, 'as draws in like' ought to be the saying, or more all utilization your sound judgment constantly, and just do what produces positive outcomes.

Being deliberate too will assist with staying away from disarray and irritations, which can both, have an unfriendly impact in your undertaking and objectives. Try not to accept work that might interfere with you.

Attempt to assess what is going on, paying a lot of significance on needs - don't stall, don't sit around idly and in particular don't squander your valuable energy. On the off chance that you act insightfully, time will be overseen most proficiently.

In the event that words, deeds, contemplations and activities are great life will be great, and every second will bring achievement and 'time' taken to accomplish the sought after objective will be… well nobody's entirely certain.

"Mind is the cause for bondage and freedom."

The Law of Success

Essentially by figuring out normal standards, of which some have proactively been examined over, one can achieve achievement.

A cognizant exertion must be made to give great encounters to the brain.

Nature has given man everything in immense overflow - tragically however people have not exactly understood this reality.

You should decide to find success. How might you do this actually?

How might you foster will? Achievement accompanies arranging, assurance and confidence no question. To learn this reality I propose that you attempt the accompanying:

Pick some genuine that you figure you can't achieve, and afterward attempt with all your energy and solidarity to do that a certain something.

There's nothing that this can't be, from attracting a picture to dominating how to utilize the PC. At the point when you have made progress, happen to something greater and keep endeavoring forward practicing your resolution. Regardless of any set backs don't be shaken by any stretch of the imagination, yet get strength from your environmental elements or more all gain from similar individuals who have looked to make progress bravely while never losing trust.

Help yourselves to remember individuals like Abraham Lincoln, Henry Portage, Mother Teresa and a lot more who have accomplished the sought after position, in view of their natural force of confidence and dynamic self control. Keep in mind, you also can make a similar progress.

This regulation can be applied by anyone and it takes care of business. The facts confirm that our contemplations and activities shape our future and predetermination. You should channel your ability and natural capacities in the correct bearing, so you can take off higher than ever.

To recap on what has been expressed hitherto, permit me to remind you the stuff to find success.

• Arranging is vital and maybe the main move toward your prosperity.

• Set yourself up to change your perspectives, propensities and your thinking designs.

• Just seek after assignments that are significant. You should separate your requirements from your needs - there is a scarce difference, so practice segregation.

• Watch what is going on. Financial plan well and decrease spending.

• Encircle yourself with individuals with a positive persona and the people who are fruitful. Peruse books about individuals who have prevailed throughout everyday life.

• Try not to profess to be who you are not. Act naturally and don't flaunt.

• Extend your viewpoint and be excited and aggressive.

• It is great to expand your pay however it is stunningly better to put resources into resources that will make you rich.

• Get ready to try sincerely and make penances.

Smart activities improve, reinforce and rouse us completely vitalizing our inward assets.

Development of such qualities and sticking to the right benefits of living will help us develop and make progress.

Such a predictable system and openness can form our personality and will assist with recovering our lower inclinations.

Time to Learn Who You Are

I would dislike anybody who might try and consider saying something, by saying that achievement is just a pie in the sky thought.

We are not conceived disappointments - let me get this point fixed. We have all been effective in our lives at some stage or another, and this is an evident **TRUTH**.

The accompanying focuses will without a doubt empower you to comprehend who you truly are, and that is an assurance. When you discover your own qualities, it turns into that a lot more straightforward to embrace goals that will permit you to jump to more prominent levels.

1. Could it be said that you are by and large excited and positive or the direct inverse?

2. Do you get a kick out of the chance to try sincerely and could you place in that smidgen of additional work on the off chance that you did what you cherish most?

3. Are you being everything that could be been - you might need to break down your assets and shortcomings.

4. Could it be said that you are satisfied with your current circumstance and additionally conditions?

After noting these three vital issues, you can decide your future. Help yourselves about the significance to remember discipline and association referenced before.

The following point I wish to feature is effortlessness. Try not to superfluously make difficulties in that frame of mind of your work and the objective to progress.

By effortlessness I mean, don't entangle circumstance, and don't allow accomplishment to get to your head - vainglorious disposition is one more issue that might cut you down. Be modest, confident and honest in your undertakings to succeed.

A quiet individual can accomplish basically anything essentially through the force of focus - this is a logical based truth.

Research has plainly demonstrated the way that strategies like yoga, perception, and unwinding can bring increased mindfulness, in this way permitting the person to arrive at his most extreme potential.

By the force of fixation and concentration, an individual can achieve what he/she has wanted.

The Need for Change

We are too mindful that nothing at any point stays extremely durable throughout everyday life, regardless of understanding one truth that life itself is a continuum, what we have neglected to acknowledge is that our own perspectives, molding and penchants prevents us from integrating changes.

One of the most troublesome things to change is our tendency (the permanent considerations), especially those that have made an imprint (outline) on our mind.

We might have the option to switch a ton of things up us yet the need to change our contemplations, perspectives and propensities which in all likelihood have turned into a piece of our self character turns out to be laboriously troublesome an undertaking.

Likewise with everything in life time can mend every conceivable thing - permit time to assist you with filling throughout everyday life and without with nothing to do arrive at your singular objectives.

How would we change our psychological demeanor? Once more the response is extremely simple - there is no confidential in that capacity, nor is this burdensome an errand to execute. The essential response lies in the word change itself. Starting progressive changes in your way of life will assist you with arriving at your objective a lot quicker. I say that the response is simple as for how we can achieve positive changes, since let us think about propensities for example

Propensities get some margin to flourish, as we are excessively mindful. Similarly as you 'learn' your propensities with time you essentially start to forget them. Propensities are undeniably challenging to destroy without a moment's delay, and hence you permit time to deal with your propensities. What has this have to do with being cheerful and rich, I 'hear' you inquire?

All things considered, my companions I might want to toss back exactly the same inquiry to you!

Wonder why you have not had the option to advance?

Set up as a regular occurrence what you have accumulated up to this point. Sit in a peaceful corner and open your heart out, and tackle this issue - the solution to all you issues positive or negative exist in you. The precision of the issue will almost certainly change, yet the reason(s) for it are obvious.

They originate from encounters, climate and your thinking designs. How can it be that individual Y can stop smoking but individual Z has a lot of hardships to stop the propensity, however both have been smoking for quite a long time, and both smoke twenty cigarettes per day? The response lies in what I have proactively talked about above, and it is our Considerations.

The one thing that you should change in your life is your ongoing view of what your identity is, others' thought process of you lastly who you truly are?

While you can change your considerations, your current circumstance and your business procedures, what you should acknowledge is that you cannot change the actual Law of Nature - it is great. Hence, we should regard this and start to stick to its overseeing elements, without abusing it. How might nature influence our prosperity?

This is a substantial inquiry, yet upon profound investigation you will comprehend that we as individuals are continually defying the norms, regulations and life's timeless cycles day to day.

Without diverging from the topic to an extreme, cautiously watch and notice how the delightful beat of nature is satisfying its obligation day to day with no conflict, and interference. Similarly we have a long way to go from Nature. Deviation from truth prompts utter disappointment and disappointment, and overstepping the Laws of Nature will bring despair - in short the cosmos and the microcosm are unconcerned.

The choices that you make in your life will decide the result of your future occasions. Continuously consider first what you are going to do or plan doing, and by embraced this act what will it then mean for you.

Try not to follow up without really thinking, but instead try to avoid panicking, calm and attempt to keep up with profound quietness however much you can. It is absolutely astounding what you can accomplish through quietness and reflection.

I truly do recommend that you embrace a type of unwinding exercise, for example, reflection or even yoga to assist you with making harmony and progress. Great judgment is an ideal mark of intelligence through the outflow of the force of keenness by means of the discriminative workforce.

In the event that you have obviously perceived your imprudence, you should concede mix-ups and vices. In the event that it disturbs others or influences your wellbeing, still, small voice, monetary status, family, prosperity and your genuine serenity, then you should ask, 'How much good would I be without it?' In the event that you don't profit from this – why indeed, even take it up or consider it?

Understanding Failure

'Reason is the greatest enemy that faith has.'

This is a reality in light of the fact that both the devotee and the non-adherent are very liable to depend on this explanation on the side of their particular contentions.

You have proactively been familiar to life's dualistic nature, and as such human explanation will find both 'upsides and downsides" for both great and atrocity separately.

This is the point at which you need to figure out how to be directed by the inward voice of 'heart'. The accompanying emerge from this natural force to be reckoned with, instinct, truth, harmony, honorableness, love, peacefulness (in words, deeds, activities and considerations) and force of segregation. These traits have their reality in the spirit.

This is the best truth that you absolutely must be aware. Exertion is relative to beauty, however I wish to add that achievement is corresponding to exertion just when you have figured out how to see the value in the characteristics of adoration.

Anything that you truly do invest all your energy and do anything that you do with outright love.

The individuals who will face challenges make progress. It is a well established truth, that youngsters are more versatile to changes. As we age it turns into somewhat precarious and harder to achieve changes and the capacity to adjust to boundless safe places. Before it turns out to be past the point of no return, remove the issue from the get-go - don't permit it chew into your framework. Like an infection make a move and eliminate it from your framework on the double.

The truth of the matter is that we are conceived great (I don't mean this from an actual perspective of the word), however the afflictions of time 'defiles' this flawlessness, and subsequently the limitless potential outcomes that falsehood sneaking inside us become diffused.

In any case, what makes us prevalent is that there is nevertheless one extraordinary and covetable gift which is our own constantly, and this is our phenomenal ability to find, create and announce that we as people have the ability to arrive at perfect in the event that not more prominent levels - existing in us is the boundless wellspring of energy that is particularly our own!

"We are helpless victims of our own desires and wants."

The Final Goal

A great many people as I'm certain you will concur do everything pitifully, and the reasons(s) for this have all been covered.

They don't utilize their maximum capacity, predominantly on the grounds that they have not figured out the force of the brain.

Frequently we are attracted or constrained to do things that bring distress. Brief joys bring distress, and subsequently larger part of us through dread or maybe even absence of certainty are 'compelled' to toss in the white towel.

This need not be the situation, since this book empowers you to conquer these obstacles, by conveying words so powerful that you can change your conditions. The time is now for you to watch the charts of your brain cautiously.

Upon thoughtfulness it is currently time to get rid of the soil and using the force of separation recognize what gives you enduring joy instead of distress.

The main concern is you need to practice command over your viewpoints.

Coming up next is incorporated to direct you to your excursion to abundance, wellbeing and satisfaction.

• Try not to harp on every one of the wrongs things you have done.

• Rehashing incorrectly activities again and again become propensities. Just make care not to rehash those moves.

• Try not to consider yourself a disappointment. Use disappointments as a way to getting achievement - don't surrender until you arrive at your ideal objective.

- You should eradicate the sections of unfortunate behavior patterns that you have made by making positive routines. On the off chance that you are lethargic choose to turn out to be emphatically dynamic and decisive - put forth yourself undertakings or objectives and ensure you accomplish them.

The way that we oppose change shows that we have our own 'usual ranges of familiarity's and this is a consequence of our viewpoints. How can it be that we oppose change - the basic solution to this question is dread of progress.

A change implies that we need to relinquish what we 'feel' is 'ideal' for us.

The inquiry then still needs to be posed is what you actually want? This is a troublesome one, and the response is that until we are not completely satisfied inside ourselves then even a tycoon who wants an additional million is a transient.

What number of us are content?

We look for moment results, and when we don't 'get' results we become discouraged and therefore surrender. It is my conviction that when you want a thing for the right reasons then nothing will at any point prevent you from obtaining it - this is the timeless regulation.

Paving Your Path to Success

I composed this book in light of just a single expectation and that is to help you comprehend and at last assist you with understanding the Force of the Psyche.

What you will presently find out is a progression of steps that you need to follow stringently to discover your firmly established want. These means are not fantastic undertakings, but rather straightforward rules to kick you off.

1. Trust in yourself, and the force of certifications. Fruitful individuals become effective through steady utilization of their self control. Try not to be scared of setbacks in the underlying stages. Change disappointments into progress through intelligence, strength and confidence.

2. Have faith in the way of thinking of 'basic living and high reasoning'.

3. Hold nothing against anybody. Endeavor to beat your previous complaints and continue on. Attempt to pardon everyone 'hurt never help of all time'.

4. Trustworthiness is the brilliant rule. Notice quietness, reflect and eliminate all regrettable inclinations from your framework (for example envy, self image, disdain, dread, etc). Adhere to the accompanying standards, love, truth, uprightness, harmony and peacefulness (you should not actually harm anybody through your discourse, activities what's more, considerations).

With relentless resolve, it is important that to gain achievement you partner with individuals who have proactively accomplished it.

To see the value in the motivation behind this book, it turns out to be imperatively critical to examine the accompanying focuses. It will sound good to you now why achievement or disappointment really relies on how you characterize yourself:

PICTURE: The better you feel about your mental self view the more probable you will succeed. Picture doesn't be guaranteed to mean looks; it likewise has a more profound significance and suggests reflection.

The picture that you might have about yourself is bound to come from your 'thought process' about yourself. The inside climate that I have examined before can assume a significant part in deciding your last objective.

FEELINGS: Clearly our contemplations and sentiments, which are unobtrusive, have huge impact in our lives. The most ideal way to check these inconspicuous powers is to practice quietness during contemplation and unwinding works out.

It is fitting to take up a type of activity to keep your brain decidedly dynamic. Obviously the subsequent advantage is wellbeing. Solid body fills in as an ideal 'vehicle' to do effectively.

Each individual looks for joy throughout everyday life. Presently the very joy we look for turns into a delight once found. This euphoria can conquer to 'delight' just by consolidating.

LOVE. You should share love in what you do and you should adore what you achieve everyday in your life. In the quietness of the evening, introspect and figure out how to work on your life (in words, deeds, contemplations and activities) and thank the preeminent general energy.

Along with what has been said above, great relational abilities, communication and great relationship is the far ahead - this is at last the embodiment of fine ideals and character that will make you effective.

Foster an amicable character, and recall what was referenced toward the beginning, consistently utilize cherishing words - words can bring harmony or begin a universal conflict.

Molding your psyche successfully will permit you to receive the benefits. It is excellent practice to examine your everyday contemplations only before sleep time, and log this in your advancement book.

Put forth objectives and targets everyday and work at it until you accomplish them.

Time is the most valuable resource throughout everyday life, use it shrewdly - time squandered is life squandered. At the point when you choose to make progress in your life, ensure you don't have clashing contemplations. Assuming that you figure out how to deliberately control and in this manner execute the boundless powers inside you, you can achieve considerably more.

Language is only the declaration of considerations and encounters.

Correspondence assumes an essential part in your general achievement, substantially less your everyday living. Through the force of information, you can accomplish explicit objectives, in light of the fact that the mystery of our solidarity is in our insight. At the point when you have a thought that is serviceable zeroing in on it hundred percent is fundamental.

Try not to enlighten the world - there is no requirement for such 'show'. Consider over it and form it into a 'item' that has a sound base. Without a strong groundwork a structure gets no opportunity to stand.

The Law of Prosperity

There is no mischief to want achievement and the wide range of various beneficial things throughout everyday life, except have confidence, want which prompts the irritating sensation of need or inadequacy can be perilous.

In the event that under any circumstance want prompts restless evenings and disappointment - the time has come to STOP whatever is it that you are doing.

Satisfaction is the genuine single component of insisting your overflow. An egotistical craving prompts utter disappointment!

Profound regulation is exceptionally strong without a doubt.

All things considered, you should attempt to follow the accompanying standards day to day in your life. Continuously take care of surrounding you, don't be tricky and underhanded.

Be careful with the self image and be valid and true.

Mindfulness is extraordinarily significant, so consistently help yourself to remember individuals who may not be so fortunate, and expand your assistance however much you can to the people who merit it.

Preparing your psyche to achieve incredible levels is definitely not a troublesome errand. In your extra time, don't squander your energy; rather invest time pondering on the force of your natural being

Reflect day to day and envision your prosperity and your objectives. My companions, the force of the psyche is absolutely wonderful, the truth of the matter is that we don't involve 10% of it in our day to day routines - presently founded on this logical seeing simply envision what you could accomplish if you somehow happened to utilize the excess 90%?

Similarly as you enjoy food when you bite it and taste it - play out every single demonstration with a feeling of appreciation and do it eagerly and in particular cheerfully.

Try not to follow every single motivation aimlessly, figure out how to reflect and recognize what is brief and temporary and what is enduring, what is fundamental and what is unnecessary, between the thing is satisfying and what is shameful.

Self-triumph will give us that which we are looking for. It must be focused on that equilibrium is likewise a fundamental fixing as you continued looking for progress and abundance. You should allot time for you as well as your family or the friends and family. A long-lasting bliss should be free of an evolving climate.

Try not to turn into an obsessive worker or a 'wealthpreneur' freak in your mission to progress, in case it harms your relationship, substantially less your endeavors to prevail in life earnestly.

Try not to veer off from the way of nobility or the Law of Nature. It is incredible fun to be sure to observe achievement and riches, and the delight that wells up is too much no question. Be that as it may, if joy, satisfaction and achievement all come on the double to the detriment of your wellbeing, then I'm apprehensive it is each of the a horrendous waste.

The best approach to being affluent, is by the work of the accompanying ideals which is our genuine real essence, and it is to be tracked down in people as well as everything around you: Truth, honesty, harmony, love and peacefulness. Ask yourself, that assuming all individual people apply these traits reliably - the world and its occupants would thrive.

We should move toward all our work (counting issues) or obligations with concentrated energy and along these lines execute it with outright flawlessness. Try to do everything (little or notwithstanding how little an obligation or occupation this might be) in an exceptional way. Play out the entirety of your work and obligation with Affection and energy, and watch the outcomes. Endeavor nothing half heatedly; you won't advance throughout everyday life.

Power of Words

Force of words can unequivocally affect our psyches and in our lives.

Before I proceed, I could like you to ponder on the accompanying inquiry, might somebody at any point stay quiet consistently?

Not telling anybody inside his/her heart and psyche for the simple explanation of not being verbally or genuinely expressive? However I can say with conviction that all of us are quiet talkers. We converse with ourselves in numerous ways and circumstances, a few times we hurt ourselves but at different times, quiet talking carries a great grin to our countenances!

Correspondence is in this manner vital throughout everyday life. Words are strong and depending how they are spoken, they can impact our everyday manners of thinking, activities, conduct and our viewpoint towards life overall.

Obviously relying upon how they are utilized the impact words can have is very staggering, they can be utilized to convince, illuminate, hurt, ease torment or even beginning a conflict! Words expressed with extraordinary feelings have the ability to bring changes that can accelerate the body's recuperating cycle!

This colossal power is in the significance of the words, what they mean to the individual who hears them. Undeniably more than straightforward correspondence, truth, deception and the boundless shades between them, words have the ability to control others' reasoning and conduct

Our understanding of words is the genuine reason for our profound responses.

Words expressed delicately, unselfishly, honestly and with outright love are the ones that get held up permanently in our being from whence they produce their mind-boggling soul blending result. Hence it is so vital to utilize words specifically and properly at some random time and circumstance.

Present day science is starting to see the value in the strong impact words can have on our bodies when they are utilized as supplications or even attestations. Did you have any idea that through cognizant exertion, we could make an exceptionally impressive resolve in ourselves?

Affirmation for success:

I will seek after tenaciously, as it is my inheritance to find true success. I'm strong and I will accomplish what I want at the time I want. I'm bound to harvest the products of my activities and I will impart my satisfaction in progress to all I know.

Benefits of Affirmations

- Confidence and an uplifting perspective
- Assists you with accomplishing objectives and targets
- Further develop you memory and abilities
- Assists with making an internal identity conviction (determination, certainty and character)
- It can assist you with advancing in a genuine way

Words verbally expressed delicately tenderly and affectionately will be alluring and obtain moment profound respect. Abundance is in itself a word, and without anyone else it amounts to nothing.

The one single variable, which gives the word abundance, the significance is the mind. The abundance of data is mysteriously gone, yet it is inside us consistently. Mind is developed through rationale, and the central matter is that dry rationale and reasoning can frequently demonstrate counter useful. Subsequently, it is fundamental to convey really, on the grounds that in quest for riches, you should sell yourself your business or your organization by means of correspondence (words).

Be that as it may, correspondence on its own won't respond your prosperity.

The Power of Unconditional Love

I can't help suspecting that individuals have failed to remember the genuine worth, significance and meaning of the word love.

You might shout and express out loud whatever has love got to do with riches! It is normally hard to characterize genuine romance, let me make sense of, say you need to figure out how to swim, you read books about the specialty of turning into a decent swimmer, yet until you don't bounce into the pool under direction, the genuine importance of swimming has no genuine worth or significance.

You should taste the natural product to know its genuine flavor, as the truism goes.

Narrow minded love established in wants that are not the slightest bit agreeable is the most harming, and in the event that you become 'submerged' in gaining your objectives through trickiness, defamation and against every one of the respectable and moral standards than you should take care of this book.

The people who comprehend love live as one and it is regular that these people will draw in what they have willed to accomplish.

The best force of fascination truly be it a relationship, business and companionship is love.

As a sprouting business visionary, recall that the appealing force of affection is unbelievable - you should rehearse empathy, and watch yourself develop and watch your endeavor flourish.

After making any type of progress in life it becomes appropriate that regardless, you don't compel your prosperity on anyone - stay away from selfishness, pride and don't force your power on anybody - it is inappropriate to do as such.

It is significant that by getting rich, you don't mishandle your recently procured 'influence'. At the point when power is utilized properly realize that you have accomplished greatness.

Conclusion

This book is composed with the view to permit you to perceive the natural inert powers that lie torpid inside each and everybody of us.

Opportunity searchers can't actually stand to 'picked and pick', but instead they ought to figure out how to benefit from all of opportunity that is stood to them.

As a searcher profit yourself to open doors that can possibly turn into vital entryway to progress - everything revolves around taking determined, controlled, estimated and an educated gamble.

Well off people have made their own profession since they are valid adherents of accomplishment.

These are people who can't stop until they make progress. They become defiant contenders just to procure their unfazed objective - they are restrained heroes using their weapons of truth, trustworthiness, genuineness, empathy, assurance, power, standards, honorableness, shrewdness, confidence, self-conviction, imagination, mettle and ability to arrive at levels second to none.

Life works rigorously as indicated by the qualities just plain irredeemable regulations. The explanation for this is to lay out proficiency, and inside the ambit of regulation, the objective keenness in man can be created to a more noteworthy effectiveness.

You are well off as of now, but because of the absence of understanding your strong natural characteristics, these traits lying in overflow have not found the dynamism to communicate and show.

At long last don't go over the top with life. Life is an excursion made workable for us all and on the off chance that we will offer ourselves the chance to develop; life can be so superb an encounter. It is generally engaging, particularly when one follows its overseeing standards strictly.

Be blissful consistently, when challenges emerge, giggle at them, and utilize the dynamic resolve inside you to ward them off. As referenced somewhere else, the body and particularly the psyche is really an astonishing instrument we have.

Condition of complete peacefulness is conceivable and there is mounting confirmation to lay out the significance accomplished by commoners from the beginning of time - it is time that you utilize the powers of your psyche to accomplish your desire(s).

www.ingramcontent.com/pod-product-compliance
Lightning Source LLC
Chambersburg PA
CBHW050312220526
45465CB00005B/1954